Caribbean Stories

Retold by Robert Hull
Illustrated by Colin Williams
and Joanne Makin

Wayland

Tales From Around The World

African Stories
Caribbean Stories
Central and South American Stories
Egyptian Stories
Greek Stories
Indian Stories
Native North American Stories
Norse Stories
Roman Stories
Stories From The British Isles

Series editor: Katie Roden
Series designer: Tracy Gross
Book designer: Mark Whitchurch
Colour illustrations by Colin Williams
Black and white illustrations by Joanne Makin
Map on page 47 by Peter Bull
Consultant: Denise deCaires Narain, Department of African
and Asian Studies, University of Sussex

First published in 1994 by
Wayland (Publishers) Ltd
61 Western Road, Hove
East Sussex BN3 1JD, England

British Library Cataloguing in Publication Data

Hull, Robert
Caribbean Stories. – (Tales from Around the World Series)
I. Title II. Series
398.209729

ISBN 0-7502-1093-1

Typeset by Dorchester Typesetting Group Ltd
Printed and bound in Italy by G. Canale & C.S.p.A., Turin

Contents

Introduction

7he Caribbean – a rich world of bright sun, brilliant flowers, delicious fruits. And of stories. Caribbean stories have always grown as easily as the colourful plants, fruits and flowers of the islands. Hardly surprising, when people came there from so many different places – Africa, the East, India, China and Europe and, later, North America.

The Arawak Indians probably came first, in deep canoes from South America. They settled in what is now called Trinidad, a few kilometres from the coast of modern Venezuela, then went slowly north, then north-west, along the whole chain of islands, as far as the Bahamas. After them came the Caribs, another Indian people.

It was a canoeful of Carib Indians that Columbus saw in 1492. He decided they were 'ignorant' and 'savage'. The Europeans' stories were soon full of the quest for gold. They saw this quest as a natural activity, and were prepared to kill to get the gold.

Soon there were few Carib Indians left; they had been killed by the Spanish explorers. And, as a result, their stories have been told less often than other people's stories.

The Spanish and then the Portuguese made up their own Caribbean stories. They brought tales from home as well, often mixing them up in a new Caribbean soup with European bits and Caribbean bits floating round together. Later the French and the British did the same, and later still people and their stories came from

China, the Lebanon and Syria, and India.

But the African population of the Caribbean is the largest. The historical true story, of how African people were brought to the Caribbean, is one of the saddest ever told. Hundreds of thousands of people were stolen from their homes in Africa, sold, and chained in dark, stinking ships for weeks. They became the slaves of British, French, Spanish and Portuguese businessmen, growing sugar-cane, or tobacco, or cocoa, or whatever could be looked after without the owner paying anything. In European eyes, and in their stories, the slaves were no more than 'lazy children'.

So it isn't surprising that in the Caribbean, African stories are the most often told. This book is full of African creatures and gods and characters. Especially Anancy, the clever, lazy, lisping, infuriating, amusing spiderman, who also came to the Caribbean in a slave ship, as a spider, or as a man, or both, or as something in people's memories.

But there are Indian Caribbean stories too, and Spanish, and French. They might all have different flavours, like the many delicious fruits of the islands – mango, coconut, banana, papaw, lime, orange. But they're all Caribbean, and as full of din and colour as the islands where your eyes meet flamingos and flying fish and flame trees, parrots and palm trees, turtles and toucans, breadfruit trees and barracuda, sour sop and scarlet ibis. And more.

There seems to be no end to the life and colour of the Caribbean. Or to the story of its stories.

After the Flood

*N*owadays Man and Woman live apart from most other creatures. They don't visit Woodpecker or Deer or Wild Pig in a neighbourly, friendly way, or get to talk to them. Human people no longer know the thoughts of creatures or understand their languages.

A long time ago it was different. Animal people and bird people and human people lived in the same villages and helped each other. Rabbit, Alligator, Toucan, Man, Woman and the rest worked together, and told each other where to find food. They all used the same language.

Then things started to go wrong. . .

One day, the big spring that brought water to the earth seemed to go wild. It began to bubble and gush up too fast, as if it would flood everything. Something had to be done. A plan was arranged. With Tiger-Cat leading the way, Rabbit, Lizard, Man, Woman and a few others went into the forest. They carried a heavy wooden lid. They fixed the lid over the foaming stream, and it slowed down. Water came to the earth at the right pace again, not too much at once, not too little.

While this was going on, Monkey was in the treetops, playing. As usual, he was looking out for fun and mischief. He heard some movement, and peering down through a banana tree saw a few creatures struggling to put a heavy wooden lid on something.

'Dey storing food!' he whispered to himself, 'A few's personal hide-hole! With special bananas and reserve mangoes! For dem only selves!'

After Tiger-Cat and the others had gone, Monkey scampered down and slowly heaved up one edge of the lid. Water leapt out. A wild, fierce creature of solid water hissed all over him. Monkey shot back and rolled over and over. He was bundled away by the rushing stream, and got left in a bush, and only just missed being drowned.

A flood spread everywhere. Water went climbing up the trees and into the hills. It flooded the fields and paths. From the foaming spring a thousand torrents gushed out over the world and covered everything. Where the forest had been, water flowed above the treetops. Alligator and Barracuda drifted through the highest branches. Nearly the whole world was water. Most of the creatures drowned.

The living crowded together on mountaintops, watching an ever-widening river swirl by with its cargo of dead. There were a few trees left. In their branches Toucan and Parrot screamed and jabbered, complaining that they had no room to roost or nest. Humming-bird had to visit the same flowers over and over again.

After a long time the flood went away. But the fields were spoiled. There were no yams, no sweet potatoes, no tomatoes. There were no little nutmeg trees. Nearly all the trees had died. There were no limes to eat, no coconuts, no breadfruit, no papaws, no oranges. Even Bee wasn't making honey. The flowers had all disappeared.

Some skilful creatures survived, eating their usual wild berries and roots in smaller amounts. But Man and Woman couldn't ever seem to find proper food, or enough of it. Gradually they grew desperate. What could they eat?

One day, as they looked round, they could find nothing on the trees and nothing in the ground. There was nothing to eat.

Man and Woman were walking by the sea. They saw Gull guarding her egg on the stony shore. A strange feeling came into them. They looked at each other.
'It's Gull's,' Woman said.

'It's Little Gull-Coming in there,' Man said.

7

They were wondering. Could they be hungry for Gull's egg? It seemed wrong, because an egg was nearly living. You could sometimes hear new birds scratching inside eggs, trying to get out. Man and Woman waited till Gull glided down to the sea, then they took the egg. They broke it, and tried to swallow. First Man was sick, then Woman, but they tried again, and it worked. They got less hungry.

They went round looking for different eggs, and started eating those too. They didn't tell any of the creatures they met, though. They knew what they would say.

Man had another thought. He said to Woman, 'If we can eat Bird-Coming, perhaps we can eat Bird.'

Man and Woman decided to try to eat Pigeon and see what happened. First they had to stop Pigeon flying, and get hold of her. They saw Pigeon dozing on a branch. They crept up and threw a net over her. Then they tried to eat. They could only eat a bit here and there, but that worked too.

After that, people caught birds all the time and had them for food.

The birds kept away from Man and Woman. They were scared. They cried in loud voices over the rivers and forests and sea-shores, 'People are taking us, taking us, taking us! Take care, take care, take care!'

Whenever Man and Woman came near in the forest, the birds fell silent. Man and Woman began to lose their skill in talking and listening to them. In a while they couldn't understand the language of the birds.

But Man and Woman wondered whether other creatures might be food. They thought of ways of catching and killing. Thinking of the way sharp stones cut into their flesh, they sharpened shells and flint and bone and fastened them to long sticks. They blew these sharpened sticks through a tube at Iguana and Wild Pig. At first they often missed the creatures. Sometimes the tips of the arrow-sticks weren't sharp enough, and they fell out. But people had learned to kill Pig and Iguana, and eat them.

More and more creatures avoided people. They were scared. Mouse would step off the path when she saw Man or Woman coming, and hide in silence till they had gone by.

Frisking Squirrel learned how to stop rock-still and be silent as a cloud. Many creatures went further into the forest to live in secret. When they met people by accident near one of their villages, they ran away.

When people went into the forest to hunt they hardly even noticed how Bell-Bird sounded a warning to the others. They didn't know the animals were lying there, silent and still, listening. They heard the monkeys scream louder, and saw the birds fly high in the air, and Rat go 'plop' down to the bottom of the river, but they didn't understand why.

Human people now had no friends. Instead, Snake slid away hissing in contempt and Jaguar crouched down in the grass, his tail whisking with anger.

Man and Woman forgot what it was like to be neighbourly and friendly with other creatures, and talk to them. They couldn't remember Parrot calling out his news of the forest, or Owl describing what kind of night he was having. They could not remember sitting down for a chat with Tiger-Cat, or Armadillo, or Alligator, or Iguana, or any of the forest-dwellers. Occasionally Donkey would still try to say something, but it came out wrong.

After many years Man and Woman no longer knew that they had once shared the world with the other creatures. They said to themselves that they lived and worked alone. They were separate, and very special. If someone had said that long, long ago human people and all the other creatures planned and worked together, Man and Woman wouldn't have believed them. Or that in the evening humans and animals and birds all used to sit round and discuss the day's events.

Separated from the other creatures, people become selfish. They also became lonely.

One day, Man and Woman were catching fish at a place in the river they often came to. It was the favourite fishing-place of Arawidi, the sun spirit.

When Arawidi saw them he thought, 'There will soon be no fish left in my river. If I help these lonely people, and make a creature-companion for them, this companion can be a friend to them and help them hunt. He will take them to other places and keep them away from my fish.'

That evening, while Man and Woman slept by their fire, Arawidi gathered up the uncooked fish they had left nearby. He quickly shaped a new creature from the fishes' cold, clammy bodies.

This new being was created to be Man's and Woman's friend. It was Dog. Arawidi gave the Dog creature a shining, smooth coat which Man and Woman would enjoy touching, and a tail for waving about. Arawidi was pleased with the creature's voice. It was bright and noisy. It would cheer Man and Woman up, Arawidi thought. Dog would never let people forget where he was.

Dog, the new creature, voiced his 'woof' and woke up Man and Woman. He licked their faces to tell them he had arrived.

On their faces his nose was cold. That was where Arawidi had held the fish while he had shaped Dog. The tail wagged and wagged. From that time, Dog always led Man and Woman everywhere and stayed patiently with them, whatever they were doing. Dog understood a few things that people said, especially if he put his head on one side and concentrated. When he replied 'woof' in different ways it sounded like different words.

Dog helped people with their hunting, going ahead and finding the track. Being wise, he also began to teach people how they once shared the world with other creatures. After a while Dog gave up. Human people were clever, but some things they would never understand.

Why Tortoise Doesn't Fly

*A*t the beginning of the world the birds and the animals weren't always sure what they should be doing on the earth. Even simple things like what noises they should make or how they should travel around hadn't been worked out.

All day long creatures could be seen trying out swimming in the river, or bounding over the plain, or crawling under rocks. Under the trees they strutted about, experimenting with whistling and cawing and hooting, then they gathered to tell each other which sound they liked best. That was the way Owl decided on his slow, hooting voice, when the others told him how well it suited his big, round eyes and the fine way he slowly turned his head right round.

One day Crow and Tortoise were watching monkeys swinging high in the sunlit trees. They were very good friends, and enjoyed walking round looking at the world. Tortoise admired Crow's shiny black coat, and Crow loved the gleaming shell Tortoise wore, which in those days was smooth enough to use as a mirror.

'At least the monkeys are trying to do something interesting,' said Crow. 'The others are all doing easy things – walking and hopping and even just creeping. There must be something really different we could do. . . Let me think . . . Hmmm . . .'

'I agree,' said Tortoise, and he started thinking too.

Crow and Tortoise sat on a log. There was a long pause while the thinking took place. Suddenly Crow

12

sprang up. 'I know! I think I'd like to go straight through the air, not go with my claws on the ground like this, scrunch, scrunch, but with my feathers out. Like this!' Crow stretched out his feathers as wide as they would go. 'Flying, that's it! No one's done that yet. It would amaze everybody. It might be dangerous, being up there in the big wind, but think of the excitement! Besides, what a way to see the world! Flying's the thing for me.'

'Me too,' said Tortoise. 'I'd love to fly. I don't know why I didn't think of it before. Floating with my feet spread out, like a leaf over everyone's head!'

The two friends told the other creatures that they had discovered a new way of travelling around. Soon they would fly like leaves in the wind.

Next day Crow and Tortoise met the other creatures and told them the plan. They were going to climb a hill and fly down from the top. They set off. The others watched from below, growing very excited. No one had flown before. They looked up towards the top of the hill, shading their eyes against the sun. Yes! Crow and Tortoise had just reached the top! There they were, right at the edge. Soon they would fly!

Everyone below waited for Crow and Tortoise to take off. There they stood, Crow with his feathers already stretched out, Tortoise next to him, stretching out one leg at a time, as far as it would go.

A few creatures below began to worry. Rat said, 'Do you think they'll really fly?'

Cat said, 'What will happen if they don't?'

Others were sure Crow and Tortoise would fly. Mouse said, 'Tortoise is wise. He wouldn't fly without thinking hard about it first.'

'Yes,' Alligator said, 'He'll make a good instructor, and teach the rest of us how to fly.'

The creatures didn't have to wait long to find out what would happen. Up on the hilltop, Crow was saying, 'Are you ready, Tortoise?'

'Ready, Crow!'

'Right then! Off!'

Out from the hill they plunged. Zoooom! Flap, flap went Crow's feathers. Wag, wag went Tortoise's short legs.

13

Crow flapped and flapped his big black wings and stayed high in the blue sky, going up and up. Crow was flying! Down below, the creatures waved their paws and screamed and cheered in excitement.

But what was happening to Tortoise? He was falling, falling, falling. Feet were no use for flying, he realized as he tumbled dizzily, dizzily, head over tail over head over tail towards the ground. Most of the creatures below closed their eyes. Cat said, 'That's what I said would happen,' even though she hadn't.

Crash! A cloud of dust splashed up where Tortoise hit the ground. When it cleared the creatures rushed over and found Tortoise lying there, rubbing his head and peering around in dismay. His beautiful, smooth, shiny shell lay in pieces all round him! At least he was alive, though. Thank goodness!

The creatures scampered about picking up the pieces. They couldn't imagine the world without Tortoise and his beautiful shell. In hardly any time at all the pieces were spread next to each other on the ground. The pieces made the complete shell. All that was needed now was to glue them together and put Tortoise's house back on his shoulders.

That is what happened. But after it was put together again the shell wasn't smooth any more. It was bumpy and cracked-looking. The joins in the shell still show where it smashed apart on the day Tortoise decided to fly.

After his accident, Tortoise was a much more thoughtful and cautious creature. He peered this way and that before he made up his mind about anything. He started to do things very slowly, to make sure nothing went wrong the way it did on the sad day he lost his smooth shell. In that way Tortoise slowly, very slowly, came to be the wisest of all the creatures.

Anancy Gets Common Sense

Anancy went looking for common sense. He wanted to collect up all the common sense there was. That way, no one else would have any. Then people with no common sense would come to Anancy with their problems and worries and would have to buy some of his common sense to help them. Anancy would get rich and be the most powerful person in the world.

Well, Anancy went around and around. He went everywhere. He peered and listened and watched. He found common sense here and common sense there and picked it all up. Anancy went along and gathered all the common sense he could find and put it into a big calabash. He collected so much common sense that he thought there couldn't possibly be any more in the world.

'Now,' Anancy said to himself, 'I'll put this stuff somewhere. I'll climb this tree and hide the calabash in the top branches.'

So Anancy tied a rope round the calabash and put it round his neck. Up he started, with the calabash on his belly, between him and the tree. Of course, it kept getting stuck. Anancy had to keep bending himself out from the tree, making space to hitch up the calabash. He grunted. He sweated a gallon. He went slowly, and then he went a lot slower. 'Some awkward stupid calabash!' he said out loud. He muttered a few more things at it.

Anancy heard a big laugh. He looked down. A small-size boy was standing there, at the bottom of the tree. 'Anancy, you put the calabash behind you! That way you climb quicker!'

'What smart small-size boy telling me how Anancy climbs?'

'You going nowhere fast, nearly backwards up there!' And he laughed again, because he was cheeky.

Well, Anancy knew he hadn't got every last bit of common sense in the world in that calabash, because a smart, no-size boy had some. And if he had some, other folks probably had too, and there was no money in selling it. Anancy knew he wouldn't be rich and he wouldn't be powerful. So Anancy got mad and pulled the calabash over his neck and threw it away.

It hit the ground and smashed. Common sense spilled out and blew all over the place. The wind carried scraps here, there and everywhere. Anybody could just pick it up, and they did. No one had all of it, but nearly everybody had some. Which is how it is. Anancy made it that way, but he didn't mean to.

The
Heron-Woman

ou heard birds calling all day long in the fishing village where handsome Damion lived. In nearby Flamingo Bay there were thousands of birds – flamingos, egrets, terns, herons and all kinds of gulls.

Damion lived with his granny, who'd raised him. He was the best-looking young man in the village, but he knew it. He had a big idea of himself. He was a big talker and a smart dresser, always smiling with the girls. For the pretty ones he'd play his guitar and keep up flattering talk, smooth as a river going along. The girls who weren't one hundred per cent pretty were nothing to him. He'd ignore them, or make cruel, jokey remarks, like 'She too heavy big-footed, she tread my foot in,' or, 'She need more hair for preference, is like stroking a coconut.'

Some of the mothers who wanted their girls married weren't put off by this big-head cruelty. He might like their daughters, they thought; he might want to marry them. So they brought him cakes and mended his smart clothes. When he passed by they called, 'Cool drink of limeade, mister Damion?' or 'A bit of tea and coconut cake, mister Damion?'

This kind of treatment made Damion even more conceited. He got more casual in how he acted. Once or twice he asked a girl to marry him; the next week he said he'd changed his mind.

'How you meaning, change your mind?' one girl asked.

18

'I mean, you less pretty this week. You're unreliable how you look.'

The girl couldn't believe the insult she was hearing. She ran off in tears.

Things like this kept on happening. To a stranger it would have seemed as if the girls were queuing up to be insulted. The cruelty of handsome Damion came to be known all through the island. No one knew what to do about him. His granny was the only one who said something straight out: 'You too smug and smirky with girls. You going get your big head drum-banged one day, you see.'

Even after his bad name spread around, young girls still fell for him. Every one of them, urged on by their mothers, hoped they'd be the one to make a kind, decent man out of him. It never worked.

Two strangers, a woman and her daughter, came to live in the village. No one knew from where. The daughter was so beautiful Damion couldn't believe it. He was used to the village girls. This one looked different, dressed differently, talked differently. Damion fell for her. The smart young man lost his cold heart within minutes of seeing her.

The mysterious woman and her daughter settled in the village, but still no one knew where they came from, or anything about them. They didn't mix with other folks, and they weren't seen much round the village. People noticed strange things about them: 'Those folks don't seem to work fields, or go to the shop much.'

One woman said, 'I never see either one buy fish. Maybe they have folks bring fish first thing in the morning.'

'I see them come back late, sometimes,' another said, 'at sunset.'

Then people saw that young Damion was wild with love for the beautiful young daughter. For a while they forgot about the couple's strange ways. 'He's on the way to being her husband if he can,' they said. 'Pity her, poor thing, marrying that Damion. But they too high-up to tell any warning to, such folk.'

And so it happened. The beautiful stranger was to marry the handsome Damion.

Two days before the wedding, Damion's wife-to-be spoke to him:

'You know, we're different, my mother and I, from these village people. You must expect to find us different. You won't complain, my lovely Damion, will you? And you be willing that my mother should stay with us?'

'Certainly she live with us, and I doesn't find you strange, not anything you does,' came the reply. Damion was dizzy-blind in love.

The next day his granny died. On her deathbed she said some strange things: 'I not wanting to see you married and marred, son. Even so I bless you, and hope and hope for you. But I glad I going be gone, and won't see it happening.'

Damion didn't stop for half a second to wonder what she was glad she wouldn't see.

Damion's marriage to the beautiful stranger was fine at first. Perhaps his granny's blessing helped Damion. All that summer he was happy. They were all away from home during the day. He sailed out

with his boat or worked at his nets, and his wife and her mother always went somewhere. At night, after sunset, his wife and her mother would make and mend their fine clothes. That was all they seemed to do. Damion didn't worry about anything, and at first he hardly even noticed anything unusual, he was so blind with loving.

A few months passed. There was no sign of a son or a daughter. Damion had begun to realize he didn't understand his wife's ways. He began to worry about things he noticed. One morning early, as his wife and her mother were leaving the house, Damion started questioning.

'Why you and your mother always leaving first thing in the dawn and not back till sunset? You never saying where you been. What you do all day?'

The answer was cool. 'Damion, you promised not to complain about what we do different to you.'

'I not complaining. I asking.'

'Well we're not answering,' his wife said. 'We're not to be cross-questioned. This isn't a law-court place.'

'But I interested what you do!'

'You're not interested, just curious and prying. We could be visiting friends. We could be going on trips to the place we came from. Anything. You'll see us after your work. There's your food, and your shirt ready.'

And off they went. Damion had to go on putting up with not knowing how his wife spent the day. There were other puzzles too. There was always food for him, but they hardly ever ate in the house with him. They didn't eat yams, or beans, or bananas, or coconut, only sometimes a bit of crab or crayfish.

Damion went round in a daze of bewilderment. He lost his big conceit and turned dark-faced and scowling. The other young men of the village, and some of the girls he'd been cruel to, weren't disappointed that Damion had problems. They'd throw remarks at him: 'Marriage ways not quite up to your liking, Damion?'

'That lady a bit high above you in talents and classy talk, Damion?'

'Them smart clothes not working the effects like they used to, Damion?'

Damion couldn't stand it any more. He decided to follow his wife and her mother, to see where they went all day.

The sky was a pale grey, with the sun still below the ridge of the hill, when Damion heard the door creak open. His wife and her mother were leaving.

He crept out after them along the track, keeping out of sight round bends or behind trees. He watched them hurry along, wondering what their strange errand could be. They were dressed in their fine town clothes, silk gowns that they held up from the dew and bits of straw on the track. They wore white lace gloves and carried parasols.

They didn't take the turning to the village. Instead, they carried on straight, towards the sea, in the direction of Flamingo Bay and the villages further along the track. 'Who they going to?' Damion asked himself. 'Maybe some secret relative sick a short distance away.'

Maybe that was why they seemed to be in such a hurry. Then, after a while, when Damion was sure they were on their way to another village, they suddenly turned off the track and headed through a tomato field,

21

straight towards Flamingo Bay. Then they started to hurry. They disappeared into a clump of bushes and small trees at the end of the field. Running hard, thinking he mustn't lose them now, Damion followed. Stumbling through the bush and throwing creepers aside, he suddenly found himself right on the edge of the bay.

The sun was just lifting over the hill and a great glitter lay on the water in front of him. The tide was going out, and birds in their thousands, it seemed, were feeding near the edge of the water. Damion put his hand up to shade his eyes against the dazzle on the water and the silver gleam of the mud.

'Where they gone? Where they gone?' he said aloud in his desperate mood. He couldn't see them. Then he saw a lace glove on the mud. It was near where about twenty herons stood round in a kind of circle, calling in harsh voices. He looked round. Other herons were walking up from the water with their long, stilting gait. Then more big, dark wings came flapping low towards the others, their shadow-wings darkening the glistening silver mud.

Damion couldn't understand. He began to be scared. Where were the two women? He walked over the sucking mud towards the glove. As he went he stared at the herons. Wings extended, they were leaping upwards and calling, with their necks and long, yellow beaks pointing straight up into the sky. Then he saw something else. Strips of silk lay on the mud amongst the birds. Then Damion saw what looked like the remains of a dress. He went up closer to see. Where were his wife and her mother?

The herons were still leaping, wings extended, like young birds ready for their first flight. Then he saw that the two birds in the centre were different, almost as different as his wife and her mother from the village people. He looked hard at them. He saw something that made him shudder. The two birds had feet that were not bird's feet, not yet. As he watched, each foot began to lose its human shape. It altered and faded, like a tide going out, and left the outline of a cruel, taloned foot in its place.

Terror flooded over Damion, and he found himself looking into the eyes of one of the two birds. The eyes he looked into were not yet flint-cold, yellow bird-eyes. They were the blue-grey eyes of his wife. But, in the very instant that he realized he was looking into eyes that he knew, the iris altered shape and colour, and the pupil narrowed to a needle-thin line. The answering gaze was blazing and merciless, a hunter's. He felt like a small crab stranded on the mud.

He started to run. Over the sucking, slowing mud, up the beach towards safety. A hundred pairs of wings flapped casually after him, and swooped heavily down at his back and head. Dark shadows whirled round Damion; beating wings nearly knocked him over. Long beaks flashed at him and tore his smart clothes. He kept running, arms high over his head, and reached the trees, where he reeled to the ground in a faint of terror.

When he came round he looked down to the water and saw hundreds and hundreds of birds feeding as before. The sun was high in the sky. Flamingos, egrets and herons were scattered all round the bay, stalking the water's edge for small crabs and eels, anything they could find.

To Damion this peaceful scene was full of horror. He now understood. This was where his heron wife and her heron mother came every day, to be with their own kind. He had married a garlin, a heron-woman. And when he found out they had tried, or perhaps only threatened, to kill him.

Damion could not go home. He could not go back to the village. He disappeared.

The village keeps to itself the story of the heartless young man who married a garlin-wife. He deserved it, some say:

'Cruel Damion found his darlin',
Married right, with cruel garlin.'

24

Anancy Wants A Money Marriage

*A*nancy always looks for help to get things done. Sometimes because he needs more cleverness than he's got on his own, but mostly because if it's a bad thing he's doing and it goes wrong, someone else gets the blame. That's how his mind goes.

Anancy wants to get married and have a lot of money. He's always looking out for a beautiful lady with a big bankful of money.

Anancy decides his chance has come when Chief says he wants his daughter to get a husband. She's beautiful, which is the right idea, but being Chief's Daughter she's rich too, which is an even prettier thought for Anancy

There's a problem. Chief has set a hard task for the man who wants to marry Chief's Daughter. Chief thought up this task long ago, when his daughter was born. 'We won't let anyone know her name,' he said, 'only palace people and private servants. When she's old enough to be married, we'll have a competition. The man who guesses her name can marry her.'

'What will we call her till then – when we're visiting round the island?' Chief's Wife said. 'We can't say "you", "you" all the time till she grows up.'

'We'll call her "Daughter" away from home. Everyone can say "Daughter".'

Which is what happened. Only Chief and Chief's Wife and the palace people and private servants knew her real name. The palace people and servants

promised never to say her name outside the palace. They swore to hope to die if they did.

Now Anancy hears about this test, and decides on some thinking. He walks up and down, considering hard.

'So, this princess's name is total hundred per cent secret outside that palace. But inside things is different. It's everybody knowing it in there. Uh-hem hem . . .'

He walks up and down some more.

'Bro Dog is my friend for this,' he says to himself. And off he goes to Bro Dog's house.

'Bro Dog, you there?' Anancy calls.

'Here I am, Nancy. How is you this sunshine morning?'

'Thoughtful, Bro Dog, is how I am. Thinking how I need you to assist.'

'Assist what, Bro Nancy?'

'Something planning in my head, Bro. You willing to assist your old, old friend to get married?'

'You coming to the top friend, Bro. I goin' be best man at your wedding with pleasure. Who you marrying?'

'You gone wrong, Bro Dog. I not marrying yet, till I get selected.'

'You still got to get selected?'

'You come down near the palace and help me get picked to marry Chief's Daughter? I'll tell you how on the way.'

'You trying tall high, Bro Nancy. Chief's Daughter! But for sure I will, Bro Nancy. Say what you planning.'

So Anancy and Bro Dog start off towards the palace.

Anancy knows a river where Chief's Daughter and girls from the palace swim and play and throw a ball around. That's where they're heading. When they get there they see the girls playing.

Anancy gets Bro Dog to roll in some river mud plus a bit of cow-muck from the track. That's so he's disgusting and to disguise him. Bro Dog is such a good friend he's willing to help Anancy in emergency work.

Anancy hides in a bush while smelly Bro Dog trots towards the girls playing ball. Nearby there's a pile of ordinary clothes and a pile of royal ones. Bro Dog saunters over and sniffs around, then lies down on the royal heap.

'Nasty dog, off away, shoo! get out of here with your nastiness! Those are Princess Basamwe's things!' And Bro Dog runs off.

Anancy hears the name. Basamwe, Basamwe.

On the way home Anancy dreams on ahead to his wedding time. 'You done help me find out her name, Bro Dog. I'll help you. Sometime soon. Husband of Chief's Daughter going to have maximum opportunities.'

'Well, I hope you right. Sounds too easy easy.'

When he leaves Bro Dog, Anancy starts to worry about it being too easy easy. He goes to see Obeah-woman in her little house, to ask her if everything's fine the way he thinks it is. Obeah-woman tells him that she'll look into it, and if he comes back tomorrow with one gold piece she'll have the information ready.

Now, Anancy doesn't like parting with money, not his own anyway. So he recalls that Bro Monkey keeps some gold coins hidden in his tree house, and goes off and skids up the tree as fast as fast. He finds the coins and permanently borrows a couple. One is to pay Obeah-woman with and one is for wedding expenses.

Off Anancy goes back to Obeah-woman. What Anancy doesn't know is that Monkey's gold belongs to Obeah-woman. Monkey is only looking after the gold pieces for her. So when Anancy pays Obeah-woman, he's paying her with her own money, stolen from Monkey, and she knows straight away.

Obeah-woman doesn't like this at all. As a result, she starts planning, the way Anancy did.

On the test day, Anancy turns up at the palace gate, in a hired carriage with horses. He gets out in his top hat and his smartest shiny suit. He has a watch with a chain and a walking-stick and bright shoes, and he's carrying a bagful of presents. He pulls on the bell.

Anancy's taken to Chief and Chief's Wife and Chief's Daughter. He starts his little song:
> 'Royal people, all of we
> in this palace, you and me,
> know the name of . . .'

Anancy pauses for big effect:
> '. . . Basamwe!'

Anancy has a first-class grin on. He's looking straight at the Princess Basamwe with it. He's never been so pleased in all his life. He's like the smartest monkey sitting on the tallest tree in the world.

Chief's Daughter doesn't seem so pleased. She's staring hard at Anancy and not smiling. Things start to happen. Anancy's hat flies up somewhere high. His stick walks away by itself – tap, tap, tap. His presents get out of the bag and unwrap and there's nothing in them. His shiny suit is in bits and shreds on the floor. Anancy's standing there in his underpants, feeling very embarrassed.

Anancy knows why everything has gone wrong. Obeah-woman must have told Princess Basamwe about Anancy's trickery. Those Basamwe eyes look like Obeah-woman's. Obeah-woman has borrowed her eyes to look through and ruin him! That's it! He runs outside. His horse and carriage aren't there.

He's running home, thinking, 'I'm only Anancy, not Chief's Daughter's Husband. I'm a no-money, no-wife spiderman.'

Anancy runs all the way home. At least his home is still there.

His cleverness is still there in his head, too. 'There'll be another time,' Anancy thinks to himself.

When The Paths Disappeared

It was the strangest thing that ever happened on the island. People said the magic of Okurri Boroku made it happen . . .

The tobacco on the estate was ready for picking, and the coffee. The sugar-cane stood tall in the fields. The sun reached through the orange trees to the houses. Long beams of light came up to the houses to wake people. The sun tapped the blinds. It seemed to be saying, 'I've started my day, I'm out in the fields. Dream's done, get along, folks!'

In the houses people tumbled round, getting themselves ready for a long day working. Wash, and dress, and eat. Get going. Set out into a dusty, hot day. Same as yesterday.

But that day no people went along the paths. No one walked down the road to the village. No one came home from visiting friends and relations. No traveller headed for the coast. Because that day there were no paths and no roads. They were lost. They had gone away somewhere. High grass and forest had come to take their place.

It was the same all over the island. People set out to work, talking, laughing, shouting. They went a short way and stopped. Along every small track, on every road and path on the island a wall of grass swayed in the wind. Tall trees stood there, full of leaf-noise like the sea, and, further on, non-stop monkey-chatter and bird-calling.

Word about what had happened couldn't spread anywhere. Not even fear could travel, or rumours about why the paths had gone.

The rich fields had vanished, overgrown with weeds and grass and undergrowth. No tobacco plant was to be seen, no coffee, no sugar-cane. Only thick, high grass and forest.

Like in a flood, people were marooned, trapped. They had to stay just where they were. Every place was an island. Nothing happened and no one called. People couldn't talk to their neighbours nearby. They couldn't even go out to look for where the paths had gone to, because the grass and forest were too thick and high. At the beginning, a few tried to escape. They disappeared.

'All you, don't go dere,' parents said to their children. 'Mister Death is yonder, stalking where the trail was.'

Not being able to go anywhere, people grew weary in their minds. They were imprisoned in their own homes. Everyone had chains on them – heavy boredom, sadness, longing for other places. Hill folk trapped at the coast dreamed of the cool mountains. Coast people, far inland, imagined the sounds of the far-off sea in the leaves and grass sighing in the wind.

Time healed nothing. Loved ones were separated. Fathers who had been working away from their own villages when the paths disappeared gave up hope of seeing their wives and children again. Many people died far from home. Hopes, dreams, and longings vanished along the lost paths. People's minds were overgrown and choked up too. No thoughts travelled far. Some people went mad.

Occasionally, people would go off into the wilderness, desperate to see another place and other people. Risking their lives seemed better than being trapped in a bad dream. For life was like a bad dream to them. Nothing changed, nothing happened.

The estate was now a tumbledown place. Creepers had swallowed the big house. The sheds had sagged-in roofs and empty windows. Turkey vultures with outstretched wings sunned themselves on house-tops. One morning, unable to face seeing all this for another

day, the owner rode off and never returned. A few days later his son set out to find him, taking some slaves. None of them ever came back, and several weeks later his wife died of despair.

For twenty years it went on the same.

Still living on the estate, after all that time, was an old African couple. No one seemed to remember their names. They had twenty sons. One by one, as the boys grew up they grew restless.

'This is a cage, father, this place. I want to break out. I want to go away, and be somewhere else.'

Whatever their mother and father said, however much they cried and pleaded, the boys left. One by one they disappeared into the wildness. They were never seen again.

Then, when she was quite old, the mother gave birth to twins, two boys who were as alike as two kidney beans. The couple were full of joy and fear at once. They knew that sometimes twins have magic powers. 'Perhaps they bring miracle strength,' the mother said. 'One of them might be a god, who knows?'

'We shall soon know,' her husband replied.

When the elders saw the twins, they realized that they were ibelles – magic twins. The elders knew because they saw a strange light surounding them. 'They have brought this light from the sky,' the elders said. 'They are princes, sent by the god Olodumare. Olodumare has sent them with light like the moon he made. He has been thinking of our sadness and wants to help.'

The couple were overjoyed – their twin sons were ibelles! Their parents called them Taewo and Kainde, and watched over them with extra-fussy anxiety. Their neighbours doted on the twins, too. They brought flowers and presents for 'our magic boys', as they called them. For the first time for many years, the people on the decayed and abandoned plantation started to feel hope.

They decided to celebrate feeling hopeful. There was dancing and feasting. The drums throbbed and sang till the long-silent air seemed surprised. The women laid out as many mangoes, coconuts, papaws and other fruits as they could find. They cooked delicious river-fish.

Their parents brought up the twins like special people. Nothing was too good for them. But in other ways the ibelles were just like the rest of the children. They played just as many tricks as they did, even more perhaps, like the kind only twins can play, when you can't tell one from the other. And at the end of the day they had just as much mud and muck on them as ordinary, messy, un-magical children.

But Taewo and Kainde slowly learned, like the others, that they lived in a dead time, in a dead place. They too saw that no one came and no one went. Nothing happened. When they were almost young men, they said, 'Mother and father, this is a cage, this place. We want to break out. We want to go away, and be somewhere else.'

They had used the same words as the other sons! They too would go away!

When their sons had gone to sleep, the couple cried and cried. 'The ibelles will go away and die, like all our other sons! What can we do?'

They could do nothing. The ibelles had come from the sky, from Olodumare. Perhaps it was Olodumare's will that they should go into the deep forest.

The other people found out that Taewo and Kainde had decided to go. There was a feast for them, but it was a feast without much festivity. No one was really hungry, and the singing was sad, like the wind drifting through hollow trees. As men and women swayed and hummed, they felt sadder and sadder. Then a blind woman stood and took the hands of one of the others. She led the dance into a circle that went leaping and swinging, the blind woman singing higher and more clearly. The dance became a strong dance of hope, and the old woman's song was joyous. The people began to feel good about the ibelles going.

When the dance ended Kainde and Taewo, the two ibelles from the sky, had gone. They had faded into the tall grasses like smoke from the fires. No one had seen how the grass opened silently in front of them, to let them through.

For seven weeks the twins wandered over the island, sleeping under the stars. It was as if they were looking for something to end the island's terrible dream.

33

Throughout their wanderings, no evil spirit dared to come near them.

On the first day of the eighth week, they came to a hillside near the sea. The hillside sloped down to a narrow, sandy beach with the sea on both sides and tall grass, forest and moutains at the other end. The twins had to cross this stretch of beach. It was the only way to get to the other part of the island. But half-way along the beach, towering nearly as high as the hill the ibelles looked down from, a gigantic, evil-looking figure blocked the way, throwing its shadow right out over the sea. The gruesome Okurri Boroku!

The twins went down on to the beach and walked towards him. From a distance they saw mounds of what looked like dry driftwood heaped all over the sand. As they came closer, they saw what the piles were. Not driftwood, but human bones. Kainde and Taewo were walking into a skeleton dump, guarded by a mountain-high ogre.

The monster's eyes were closed. He was asleep. But he was terrifying just dozing. A moaning, whistling sound came from his mouth, which sagged open like a horrible purple flower. The twins gazed up at a square face that was the same white as candle-grease, riddled with red veins and blotched all over. He had long, dirty, saw-like teeth, stumpy yellow wings, and dusty scales over the rest of him. Ropes of matted hair, with string and feathers for decoration, hung off him.

The twins had to get past him or give up their search. They had either to get the monster's permission, or get him.

'You! You up there, let us past!' Kainde shouted 'Please!'

Not an eyelid flickered.

'Wake up! Wake up!' shouted Taewo. 'Sir!' he added.

Okurri Boroku shuddered in his sleep, as if he'd swallowed something nasty in a dream. The whole beach trembled.

The demon snoozed on. Kainde yanked hard on one of the feathery ropes. No answer. Taewo took a thick stick and cracked it on the demon-giant's bare shin. The stick snapped. The monster didn't even bend down to scratch. Then the twins took their drums and beat them and beat them. They drummed for hours and hours. Finally Okurri Boroku woke.

'Will you let us past, please? We have waited many hours for you to wake up.'

'Many hours?' said Okurri Boroku, rubbing an eye. He looked down and roared an ear-splitting laugh. The hillside shook. Behind him flocks of birds took off from the tops of trees and flew screaming out to sea. Monkeys went howling up the hill behind.

The giant-devil's eyes were hardly open. He had seen only one of the ibelles. Taewo had an idea, and slipped off into the grass.

'I have been asleep for years!' the monster said. 'And the first edible thing I see when I wake has actually been trying to wake me! A mouthful of midget person going ting ting with his toy drum!'

He roared again, finding the idea so funny that he snorted and shot flames out of each nostril. The sand on the beach swirled round in the fierce blast. The ogre's great body was straining so hard with laughter that the twins could hear the crink-clink of twisting dragon-scales.

'I never heard such a joke! Being woken for my breakfast by my breakfast . . .' He laughed again.

Kainde was terrified. But he still had the courage to ask, 'Will you let us past?'

'Yes but. Yes but. In other words, only if. Only if,' Okurri Boroku said, 'only if you can play the guitar so well that I dance to your tune. Only if you make me dance and dance and dance till I drop. Only if you can do the impossible! Hargh, hargh!' And as he sniggered at his own words he pulled a gleaming black guitar from a kind of bag he wore around his neck. 'Play now! Play for the devil, boy! Play!'

Kainde started playing the wildest tune he knew, with the fastest words. The devil swayed and swung. He stamped and stamped, faster and faster. The valley swayed and shook too. The devil grew hotter and hotter. After a while his hair began to smoke. Steam came out of his ears. 'This is the music for me. Very good! Hot rhythms! Very good breakfast music! Play, boy, play!'

And on Kainde sang and played, for hours and
hours, till his arm ached and his throat was dry.

'I have a great thirst, Ogre-ous Sir,' Kainde said.
'Can I have a drink at the stream, please? Then I will
play again.'

'Quick then, quick!'

Kainde slipped away into the tall grass.

In a few moments the same wild song began again.
The same song, but not the same singer. It was
Taewo's hand on the strings. He had been hiding in the
grass and he and Kainde had changed places. The way
they used to at home, making fun of their friends.
Perhaps the twins could go on playing and changing
places, and on, and on, and on, without Okurri
Boroku noticing.

Taewo played and played. The devil danced to
Taewo's tune till sparks flew from him, leaping from his
teeth and his hands and his shoulders like sparks from
a grindstone. He was lit up. He was like a tower of
writhing lightning. He was going wild-dance-mad,
twitching this way and that like a ray of sun on the
water. There was no way he could keep on going.

Perhaps Okurri Boroku was a bit out of practice, Taewo thought. The devil wasn't completely fit. He'd been asleep for too long.

After a few hours, Taewo said, 'Water, sir. I need a little drink to keep up my entertaining.'

'Drink! Drink! You drink, I dance!' Okurri Boroku cried. But he was glad to stop for a minute.

In no time Kainde was back with his fresh playing-arm, crowding the beats out of that old black guitar till the strings got hot. Okurri Boroku sang the highest notes he could. His rope-like hair, with its ribbons of string and feathers, was standing up on its own over his head, swaying round with him like an upside-down jellyfish. Long, multi-coloured flames and steam shot out from both ends of the devil, and from his middle, too. He made some bells start jangling somewhere inside his scaly covering.

'Devil man, I'm going for a drink!' shouted Kainde above the din of the devil's dancing.

Taewo came back again, beating the guitar hard. Kainde rested.

It was nearly night now. A big moon came up. The guitar glistened as Taewo hit the strings. The beats thumped out over the sea, and echoed high into the forest. Then the bats came out to join in, flittering and jinking round Okurri Boroku's head. Owls swooped down and hooted around, and a crowd of other night-birds followed them. The piles of bones began to stir. Skeleton after skeleton crackled to its feet and went jittering slowly round in the moonlight. Then they speeded up, and soon the valley was lit with a crowd of silvery shapes swaying and jumping. Skeletons aren't natural dancers, and they bumped and jangled into each other and tripped up. But it was a good dance.

Okurri Boroku put extra energy into dancing with the night creatures and the raving skeletons. Then after a few hours Taewo said, 'I need some cool moonlight water,' and went off.

Kainde came back and played faster than ever. By this time Okurri Boroku was beginning to have trouble breathing. His forked tongue hung down, and his eyes looked stretched and finished. As he struggled for breath he kept a ghastly devil-grin on his face.

His mouth was pulled up over his gums, so the lengths of his great, dirty teeth were uncovered.

'While the music plays, the devil dances!' Kainde shouted.

Okurri Boroku wobbled and teetered about, but the thumping beat of Kainde's guitar drove his feet on and on.

A few more hours went by. It was nearly midnight in the blue valley full of leaping bones. As the tired old devil-giant twitched and leapt around, smaller flames came from him, and the little lightnings no longer played round him. He went slower and slower, his scales crackling, and his red eyes popped further out on his larded-up forehead. He looked a sight, even for a devil.

Suddenly he toppled over. Ker-ash! The noise was like a hundred houses coming down at once. A cloud of dust swirled up over the moon. Owls and bats flew in crazy patterns and vanished. It took an hour for the sky to clear.

By that time Kainde and Taewo had climbed the hill. They looked back. There lay Okurri Boroku, his face to the moon. He was finished as a devil. The ibelles had driven the life out of him.

Okurri Boroku was no longer standing in anyone's way. The curse was lifted. The paths and roads began to reappear.

When Taewo and Kainde were back at home, they asked Obatala, Olodumare's first god, for another thing: 'Obatala, you who make your worshippers prosperous and healthy, we ask one great thing from you where you sit in your palace with walls whitewashed like the moon. We ask you to bring back all the lives Okurri Boroku took away. We ask you to travel the paths and roads that Okurri Boroku blocked, and give life to the skeletons who lie unburied there.'

Obatala did what the ibelles asked. So the ibelles brought back not only the island's paths and roads, but also all the people who had disappeared along them.

Since that time, longings and hopes and desires travel freely over the island. And when people sit round under the moon, and the guitar sings, the paths themselves remember.

39

The Story Without An End

*T*here was once a chief who had a daughter, his only child. She grew up to be beautiful, and young men in every village wanted to marry her.

The chief liked the idea that so many fine men admired her and said they loved her. On the other hand, he didn't want her to get married, because then she would leave him. He hated the thought of living alone in the big palace without her. He liked talking to his daughter better than to anyone. No official wise person or clever joker or anybody was half as interesting.

So the chief thought up an impossible test. He declared, 'My daughter shall marry the man who can tell me a story with no ending.'

The chief said to himself, 'There's no such thing as a story without an ending. And even if some smart-brain young man thinks he knows one, and tries to tell it to me, he won't be able to finish it – if it really has no ending. Whatever happens, my lovely daughter will stay at home with me.'

Young men came from all over the island to tell their stories. The stories were thrilling and magical, but all the tellers failed the test because their tales all came to an end. Sometimes these endings seemed to come into the story by accident, without the story-teller meaning them to. Either the foul monster was suddenly killed by the hero, or the hidden treasure was found by the hero, or the newly married hero-husband and heroine-wife started to live happily ever after.

40

It seemed as if each teller enjoyed his story so much that he thought he was the hero in it and did something wonderful, so the story came to an end. So they all lost. The test beat them.

A few days after the defeated young men had left the palace, a stranger arrived. He was handsome like the others, and he had a determined, cunning expression in his eyes. 'I wish to tell the chief my story. It has no ending,' he said.

The chief groaned under his breath: 'Not another of them!' But out loud he said politely, 'A hundred young men took the test, and they all failed. It would be better if you didn't waste any more of our royal time.'

'Chief, you have invited any young man who loves your beautiful daughter to come to your palace and tell a story. I have answered your invitation. Now, can I tell you my story with no ending?'

The chief realized he was breaking his promise and being unfair, so he agreed to listen. 'Very well, tell us your never-ending story, and we can see how long it takes!' He smiled at his little joke.

The young man began:

'One morning when the sun came up, a blackbird flew down to nibble at some ripe bananas hanging on a tree by a house. A woman came out of the house and shooed the blackbird off. Then she went inside again. A little later a different blackbird came down and nibbled at the bananas. After a while the woman came out again and shooed the blackbird away. Another blackbird came down and nibbled at the bananas. The woman came out and shooed this other blackbird away. She went inside. Another . . .'

'Wait!' cried the chief. 'I'm getting tired, and it's been a long day. Come back tomorrow and finish your story then.'

'With pleasure, Chief. Tomorrow I will come back and go on with my story.'

The next day the young man come back to the palace. 'You may continue,' said the chief.

'With pleasure, Chief. Now, let me see, where was I? Ah yes. The woman had just gone inside. Right. Well, then another blackbird flew down and started to nibble at the ripe bananas. The woman came out and shooed the blackbird away. Then she went inside. Another blackbird came down and nibbled at the bananas. The woman came out and shooed it away. She went inside. Then another blackbird came down and nibbled the bananas. The woman came out and shooed it away. She went inside. Another blackbird came down and nibbled the bananas. The woman . . .'

'Stop! Stop! If that woman comes out again she'll shoo the wits out of my head! Your story's nibbling my brains away! I shall go mad!'

'But my story isn't ended, Your Majesty . . .' The young man seemed to be protesting, but he had a smile on his face.

'I know, I know. You've won, you've won. You've passed the test. Your story has no ending. It could go on till the end of the world, or even longer. Marry my daughter, take my lovely best friend away from this palace to her own home somewhere else, but please, no more blackbirds or bananas!'

So even though the story didn't end, the story of the story did.

Bro Nancy
And
Bro Death

It is a fine, sunny day. Bro Nancy and Bro Death are going to plant beans and yams. It's hard work. Any work is a mile too hard for Bro Nancy. He sneaks off into the cool shade and lets Bro Death plant yams and beans.

'Bro Death can plant all the yams and beans he can plant,' Bro Nancy says to himself.

And so it goes on. Bro Death goes 'Shu, Shu' with his hoe all day and Bro Nancy sits under a mango tree, playing the fool and pretending he's the boss: 'Do this, do that. Plant deeper'. It makes Bro Death mad. It's his field and Bro Nancy's field together, but here's Bro Nancy fooling with nonsense while Bro Death does all the planting.

'Well, no yams and no beans is what Bro Nancy's supper will be,' says Bro Death to himself. 'But lots of beans and lots of yams for Bro Death. And soon.'

Bro Death waits a few months for the field to get ripe. The beans and yams come up where Bro Death has planted them, but not in Bro Nancy's part of the field. Bro Death's yams and beans look good. Seeing them makes Bro Nancy hungry.

In a while Bro Nancy's really hungry. He says to his wife, Tookooma, 'Listen, wife, tonight I'm picking beans. Tomorrow night I'm picking yams. So hand me that basket and come and watch by the gate. We'll be eating well soon.'

'Husband Nancy, don't you go out in the dark time.

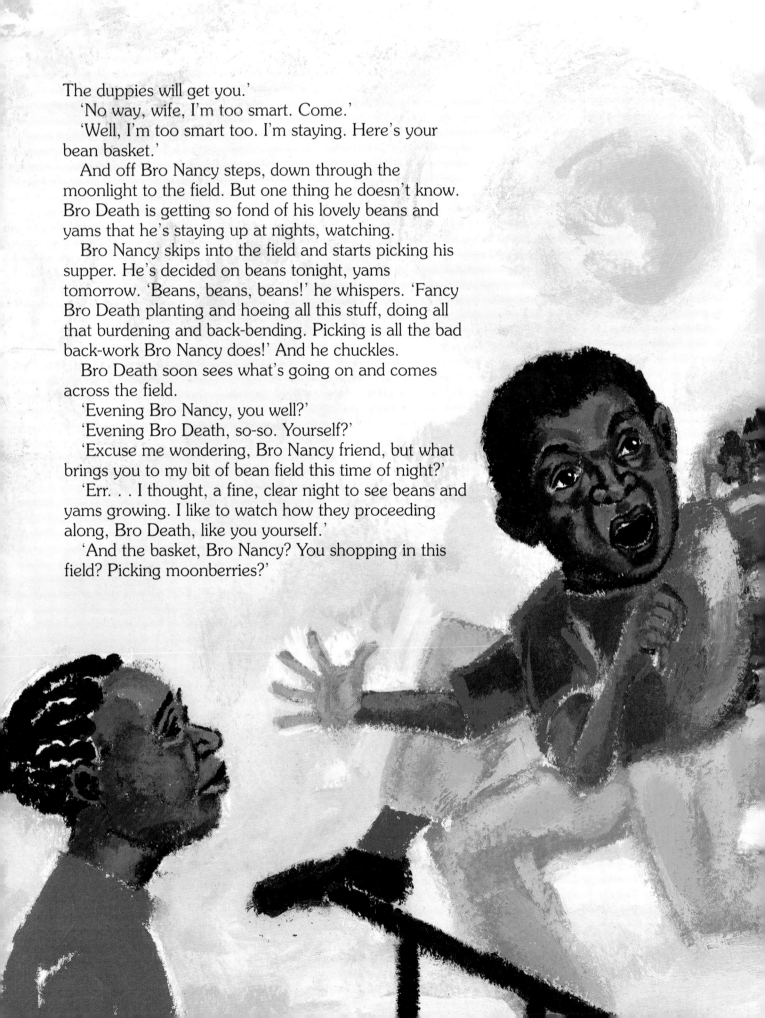

The duppies will get you.'

'No way, wife, I'm too smart. Come.'

'Well, I'm too smart too. I'm staying. Here's your bean basket.'

And off Bro Nancy steps, down through the moonlight to the field. But one thing he doesn't know. Bro Death is getting so fond of his lovely beans and yams that he's staying up at nights, watching.

Bro Nancy skips into the field and starts picking his supper. He's decided on beans tonight, yams tomorrow. 'Beans, beans, beans!' he whispers. 'Fancy Bro Death planting and hoeing all this stuff, doing all that burdening and back-bending. Picking is all the bad back-work Bro Nancy does!' And he chuckles.

Bro Death soon sees what's going on and comes across the field.

'Evening Bro Nancy, you well?'

'Evening Bro Death, so-so. Yourself?'

'Excuse me wondering, Bro Nancy friend, but what brings you to my bit of bean field this time of night?'

'Err. . . I thought, a fine, clear night to see beans and yams growing. I like to watch how they proceeding along, Bro Death, like you yourself.'

'And the basket, Bro Nancy? You shopping in this field? Picking moonberries?'

'Bro Death, friend, truth is, I'm fishing. I'm on my way to the river for crayfish. My wife said, "A little basket of crayfish would be nice for supper, husband Nancy." So here I am.'

'Fishing? Well now, I was thinking of a little fishing too. You heard of a smart little fresh fish, called "false fisherman-man", Bro Nancy, and sometimes he called "bean-stealer", Bro Nancy? I show you how to catch one!'

And Bro Death whips out a cutlass. He chases Bro Nancy. Over the field they go and up the road toward Nancy's house.

'Open that door, wife! Death's after me! Open that door!' Nancy screams as he gets near. Bro Death is catching up on Nancy, waving his cutlass and shouting, 'I'll get you! Stealing my new beans! You old spiderman!'

'Open that door, wife! Death's catching up to me!' And Bro Nancy whizzes inside his house through the door. 'Close that door, wife! Close that door! Keep Death out! Open that shed door, wife! Open that shed door!'

All this 'open the door, close the door, open the door' is confusing, but it's what Nancy's wife does, just in time. Bro Death stands outside in the moon, wafting his cutlass, like an agitated crab. 'You keep away from my beans and yams, Bro Nancy! Or Bro Death'll get you!'

Bro Nancy's already in the shed, though, climbing spider-fast up out of sight. He disappears up in some old, webby dust and dark hanging stuff and stays there. No one sees Nancy for weeks and months. He lives in a dark cranny and seldom comes out.

And that's why you find Nancy Spiderman hiding in gloomy sheds and dark nooks up in the rafters and such secret places like that.

Notes

Anancy (or Anansi or Ananse) (**say An-nan'-see**)
(p. 5, 16-17, 25-9, 43-6)
The trickster spiderman. He is the central character in many African and Caribbean stories. He is lazy and clever, and speaks with a lisp. Sometimes he is called Nancy, though that word might not come from 'ananse' meaning spider, but from 'nansi' meaning chameleon. The two words are now mixed up, though.

Arawak (**say Ah'-rah-wak**) (p. 4,5)
The Arawak Indians were probably the first inhabitants of the Caribbean islands. They came from the mainland of South America.

Arawidi (**say Ah-rah-wee'-dee**) (p. 10, 11)
The Arawak sun spirit.

Barracuda (p. 5, 7)
A fish that can grow up to nearly three metres long. It has a big lower jaw like a pike. Fishermen fear it even more than the shark.

Breadfruit (p. 5, 7)
A tree that grows up to twenty metres high and produces a large, yellowy, starchy fruit that normally needs cooking.

Bro (p. 43-6)
Like 'Brer', this word is used to speak to someone in a friendly, familiar way. It may be short for 'brother', but some people say the word is really 'bor' (as in 'neighbour'). In Barbados people still use 'bo' (eg 'I don't know, bo') in everyday speech.

Calabash (p. 16-17)
The hollow shell of a pumpkin or gourd (a type of fruit).

Carib (p. 4, 5)
After the Arawak, the Carib Indians were probably the second Indian people to settle in the Caribbean islands. The word 'Caribbean' comes from 'Carib'.

Cocoa (p. 4)
This comes from the cacao tree. Clusters of flowers ripen into yellow or red pods filled with white cocoa beans.

Columbus (p. 4)
Christopher Columbus was a fifteenth-century Italian explorer. He was the first European to visit South America and the Caribbean. He settled in Portugal in 1478, then went on his travels wih support from the Spanish king.

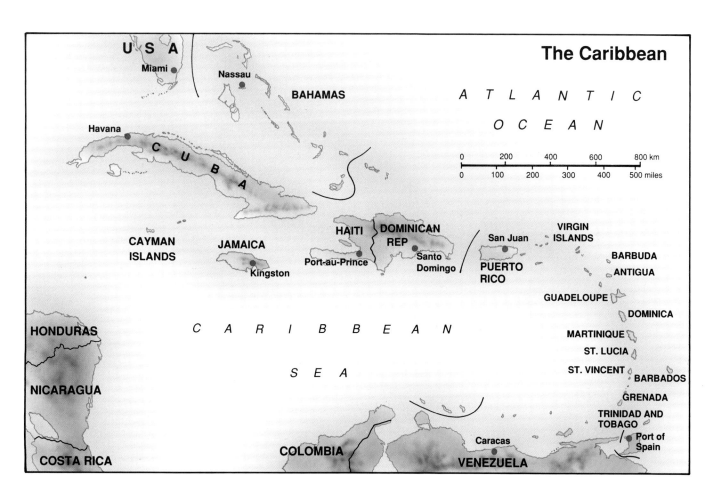

Crayfish (p. 21)
A shellfish like a small lobster, that lives in fresh water.
Cutlass (p. 46)
A curved, one-edged sword.
Duppies (p. 44)
Spirits or ghosts.
Egret (p. 18, 24)
A kind of heron, white in colour and smaller than the grey heron.
Flame tree (p. 5)
A large tree with brilliant scarlet flowers. Another name for it is 'flamboyant'.
Garlin (p. 24)
A heron.
Humming-bird (p. 7)
There are many species of these highly coloured little birds, which can hover like bees, wings beating at high speed. They live on all the islands.
Ibelles (p. 32, 33, 34, 35, 39)
Magical, sacred twins.
Mango (p. 5, 32)
An Indian tree that produces delicious, juicy fruit.
Monkeys (p. 6-7, 12, 30)
There are monkeys on Barbados and a few other islands.
Nutmeg (p. 7)
A small evergreen tree that produces a yellow fruit. The inside of the fruit is nutmeg, the case is another spice, mace.
Obatala (say Ob-ah-tah'-lah) (p. 39)
The first god to be created by Olodumare, the chief god of the Yoruba.

Obeah-woman (say Ob-ay'-ah) (p. 27, 29)
A type of witch. Obeah is a form of African witchcraft.
Olodumare (say Ol-od-yoo-mah'-ray) (p. 32, 33, 39)
'Great Everlasting Majesty', the chief god of the Yoruba people. The Yoruba people came from Nigeria, and those who were enslaved went mainly to Cuba.
Palm tree (or coconut palm) (p. 5)
This grows up to thirty metres high, generally on sandy shores. Coconuts can float, so the coconut palm has spread to all the islands.
Papaw (p. 5, 7, 32)
A large, juicy fruit that grows on a tree-like plant about eight metres high.
Scarlet ibis (p. 5)
A brilliant scarlet, long-beaked, long-necked fishing bird. It is the national emblem of Trinidad.
Sop (p. 5)
Bread dipped in soup or milk.
Tern (p. 18)
A sea bird with a long, forked tail. Terns are smaller than seagulls.
Tiger-cat (p. 6, 7, 10)
Sometimes called an ocelot, this wild cat is about twice the size of a big domestic cat, and lives high on the mountain slopes of Trinidad, the island closest to South America.
Toucan (p. 5, 6, 7)
A brightly coloured bird with a huge beak used for crushing fruit.
Yam (p. 21, 43, 44)
A large, potato-like vegetable.

Further Reading

Anancy Spiderman – Twenty Caribbean Folk Stories, James Berry (Walker Books, 1989)

Storyworlds 1 and 2, Richard Brown (Longman, 1988)

Under the Story-teller's Spell–Folk Tales from the Caribbean, edited by Faustin Charles (Puffin, 1991)

The Caribbean, John Griffiths (Wayland, 1989)